Bee-A-Treez
A picture book about
Self-Mastery
SUZY ADRA, PHD

To all the children ...

This is the story of Bee-A- Treez the Bumble Bee.

Bee-A-Treez learned to be the master of her mind and body in a beautiful and magical way.

Master of her brain. master of her arms and legs...
and everything else in between.

Bee-A-Treez lived long ago in a land far away. Her mama taught her how to make honey from the nectar of flowers.

One day while she hopped from flower to flower making honey she met a mama bird.

Mrs. bird had lost her babies! Bumble bee was too busy making honey to notice that mama bird was worried.

Wise turtle was strolling slowly by and noticed mama bird's despair. Turtle said to Bee -A- Treez "you know you probably already had enough honey. Why don't you be a master of your need for more honey and go help mama bird?"

.

Bee a Treez thanked wise turtle and buzzed around the garden looking for mama bird's babies.

Soon they were found! She found them hidden in a green bush. She called mama bird to see them.

Hooray! The babies will soon hatch with their mama around.

Bee-A- Treez felt very proud of herself that night.

The next morning was for more honey gathering.

This time a snake was around looking for breakfast too.

Bee-A- Treez watched as snake ate an entire moth in one big gulp!
!
Bee-A- Treez was furious!
What ?
That snake needs to be taught a lesson.

She flew towards the snake to teach it a lesson, but wise turtle showed up just in time.

" Bee-A- Treez what are you doing?!" asked Turtle

Bee-A- Treez answered "I want to teach snake not to eat others. I will sting it."

Turtle said "Calm down and think a little bit."
Bee-A- Treez thought for a moment...

"Well I could talk to snake instead of sting it I suppose?"

Turtle smiled and said "go on then go talk to snake."

Bee-A- Treez chatted with snake for what felt like a very long time.

She learned that snake has to eat to survive. Snake can't have honey like bee and it must eat insects to live.
Bee-A- Treez was glad she had the chat and that she was the

master of her mind and body
and did not sting snake instead.

She and snake became
really,,really , good friends.

The End

19

About the Author

Suzy Adra is an artist, certified yoga instructor, energy healing practitioner, and trauma release practitioner. She facilitates somatic movement and creative process workshops that inspire to embrace one's creative abilities. Suzy has written articles for yogapedia.com and published several articles for the Journal Challenging Organizations and Society- reflective hybrids. She is the founder of **Bīja Healing Sanctuary in Rocca Massima, Italy** and the creatress of *ArtkeyTypes*, a therapeutic psycho-somatic painting process. She holds a Ph.D. from the California Institute of Integral Studies. Her dissertation is entitled: *The States of Presence and Insight in the Painting Process.*
www.suzyadra.com

This is her second book.

21

Lightning Source UK Ltd.
Milton Keynes UK
UKRC041015010422
400892UK00001B/9